PRAYER

PRAYER

OUR DEEPEST
LONGING

RONALD ROLHEISER

Franciscan
MEDIA
Cincinnati, Ohio

RESCRIPT

In accord with the *Code of Canon Law*, I hereby grant my permission to publish *Prayer: Our Deepest Longing*, by Ron Rolheiser, OMI.

Most Reverend Joseph R. Binzer
Vicar General and Auxiliary Bishop
of the Archdiocese of Cincinnati
Cincinnati, Ohio
June 27, 2013

The permission to publish is a declaration that a book or pamphlet is considered to be free from doctrinal or moral error. It is not implied that those who have granted the permission to publish agree with the contents, opinions or statements expressed.

Cover design by John Lucas
Cover image © Masterfile | F. Lukasseck
Book design by Mark Sullivan

LIBRARY OF CONGRESS CATALOGING-IN-PUBLICATION DATA
Rolheiser, Ronald.
Prayer : our deepest longing / Ronald Rolheiser.
pages cm
Includes bibliographical references.
ISBN 978-1-61636-657-5 (pbk.)
1. Prayer—Christianity. I. Title.
BV210.3.R65 2013
248.3'2—dc23
2013021239

ISBN 978-1-61636-657-5

Published by Franciscan Media
28 W. Liberty St.
Cincinnati, OH 45202
www.FranciscanMedia.org
www.AmericanCatholic.org

Printed in the United States of America.
Printed on acid-free paper.
15 16 17   5 4

CONTENTS

PREFACE

S PIRITUALITY IS AS real as science. But that is not easy to understand or believe. We live in a world where what is real has been reduced to what is physical, to what can be empirically measured, seen, touched, tasted, and smelled. We live in a world that is for the most part spiritually tone-deaf, where all the goods are in the store window, digitized, or reduced to a flat screen. And so, prayer is a struggle. So are a lot of other things. When the surface is all there is, it is hard to be enchanted by anything, to see depth, to be deeply touched by poetry, faith, and love. But these are what we long for: depth, poetry, faith, love.

Indeed we are made for love. We are made for intimacy with each other and with God. As St. Augustine put it, "You have made us for yourself, Lord, and our hearts are restless until they rest in you." But the deep meaning of our longing is not always so obvious. Today most of us do not see our restless longing as pushing us toward the infinite. We have trivialized and tamed our longing. Instead of longing for the transcendent, we anesthetize and distract ourselves by focusing our desires on the "good life," on sex, on money, on success, and on whatever else we think everybody has. There is nothing inherently bad about these things, but if we define our deepest longings as directed toward these things in themselves, we end up mostly disappointed and empty. Our disquiet persists and we remain restless and tired, drained of energy, rather than in a place of solitude where our very striving gives us energy.

Ultimately, our restless aching is a yearning for God. We need to connect with God. We need prayer. We know this, both in our more reflective moments and in our more desperate moments. It is then that we feel our need for prayer and try to go to that deep place. But given our lack of trust and our lack of practice, we struggle to get there. We do not know how to pray or how to sustain ourselves in prayer.

Whether you struggle to even believe in prayer, are a beginner in prayer, or are more advanced in prayer, my hope is that these reflections will encourage you in your practice of prayer. This is not a manual; there are many fine books in print that teach the various methods of prayer. This is a collection of reflections that draws from Scripture, ancient and modern writers, and my own experience. Although the reflections have been arranged a certain way, they may be read in any order. Let your own experience be your guide. Trust it, trust God's providence, and trust that the text you most need to read will find you.

There is no bad way to pray and there is no one starting point for prayer. All the great spiritual masters offer only one non-negotiable rule: You have to show up for prayer and you have to show up regularly. Everything else is negotiable and respects your unique circumstances.

These reflections are intended to help you get beyond some of your habitual struggles with prayer, so that it no longer feels as though you are simply doing some drab duty, wasting precious time, talking to a wall, entertaining yet another daydream, or simply rehashing your heartaches and headaches. The reflections will try to offer a healthy combination of consolation (everyone struggles with prayer) and challenge (we all need to ground ourselves more deeply through prayer). Mostly, though, they will try to help open you so that in the most intimate part of yourself you can more clearly hear God and others say: "I love you!" For only that can make us whole.

There is a beautiful text in the Gospels that captures, in a stark metaphor, our need for prayer. One morning, after Simon Peter, James, and John have "toiled all night" and caught nothing—no fish, only their own emptiness—Jesus comes to them and invites them to go out to the deeper waters, to "put out into the deep." They do, and they catch so many fish their boat begins to sink. (Luke 5:1—7)

The reflections on prayer in this book are an invitation that echoes that invitation from Jesus: When we are catching nothing but our own emptiness, it is time to "put out into the deep."

CHAPTER ONE

Struggling in Prayer

Too Busy to Bow Down

WE ARE NOT, by choice or ideology, a culture set against solitude, interiority, and prayer. Nor are we, in my opinion, more malicious, pagan, or afraid of interiority than past ages. Where we differ from the past is not so much in badness as in busyness. Most days, we don't pray simply because we don't quite get around to it.

Perhaps the best metaphor to describe our hurried and distracted lives is that of a car wash. When you pull up to a car wash, you are instructed to leave your motor running, to take your hands off the steering wheel, and to keep your foot off the brake. The idea is that the machine itself will suck you through.

For most of us, that's just what our typical day does to us—it sucks us through. We have smartphones and radios that stimulate us before we are fully awake. Many of us are texting friends, checking Facebook and e-mails, watching the news, or listening to music or talk radio before we even shower or eat breakfast. The drive to work follows the same pattern: stimulated and preoccupied, we listen to the radio, talk on our cell phones, and plan the day's agenda. We return home to television, conversation, activities, and preoccupations of all kinds.

Eventually, we go to bed, where perhaps we read or watch a bit more TV. Finally, we fall asleep. When, in all of this, did we take time to think, to pray, to wonder, to be restful, to be grateful for life, for love, for health, for God? The day just sucked us through.

Moreover, prayer is not easy because we are greedy for experience. The spiritual writer Henri Nouwen put this well: "I want to pray," he once said, "but I also don't want to miss out on anything—television, movies, socializing with friends, drinking in the world." Because we don't want to miss out on any experience, prayer is truly a discipline. When we sit or kneel in prayer, our natural craving for experience feels starved and begins to protest.

Ironically, most of us crave solitude. As our lives grow more pressured, as we grow more tired, and as we begin to talk more about burnout, we fantasize about solitude. We imagine it as a peaceful, quiet place, where we are walking by a lake, watching a sunset, or smoking a pipe in a rocker by the fireplace. But even here, many times we make solitude yet another activity, something we do.

Solitude, however, is a form of awareness. It's a way of being present and perceptive within all of life. It's having a dimension of reflectiveness in our daily lives that brings with it a sense of gratitude, appreciation, peacefulness, enjoyment, and prayer. It's the sense, within ordinary life, that life is precious, sacred, and enough.

How do we foster solitude? How do we get a handle on life so it doesn't just suck us through? How do we begin to lay a foundation for prayer in our lives?

The first step is to "put out into the deep" by remaining quietly in God's presence in solitude, in silence, in prayer. If it is your first time doing this, set aside fifteen minutes for prayer. In time, you might be able to manage thirty minutes. (See the appendix for simple guidelines to help you begin to rest in God's presence.)

Remember: Your heart is made to rest in God. If St. Augustine is right, and he is, then you can count on your restlessness to lead you into deeper prayer—the kind of prayer that leads to profound transformation, the kind of prayer that will not leave you empty-handed.

Struggling with Boredom

Prayer has a huge ebb and flow. When we try to pray, sometimes we walk on water and sometimes we sink like a stone. Sometimes we have a deep sense of God's reality and sometimes we can't even imagine that God exists. Sometimes we have deep feelings about God's goodness and love, and sometimes we feel only boredom and distraction. Sometimes our eyes fill with tears and we wish we could stay in our prayer-place forever, and sometimes our eyes wander furtively to our wristwatches to see how much time we still need to spend in prayer.

We nurse a naïve fantasy both about what constitutes prayer and how we might sustain ourselves in it. What often lies at the center of this misguided notion is the belief that prayer is always meant to be interesting, warm, bringing spiritual insight, and giving the sense that we are actually praying. Classical writers in spirituality assure us that, though this is often true during our early prayer lives when we are in the honeymoon stage of our spiritual growth, it becomes less and less true the deeper we advance in prayer and spirituality. But that doesn't mean we are regressing in prayer. It often means the opposite.

Here's an analogy that might encourage you when you are struggling with boredom and the sense that nothing meaningful is happening:

Imagine you have an aged mother who is confined to a nursing home. You're the dutiful child and, every night after work, for one hour, you stop and spend time with her, helping her with her evening meal, sharing the events of the day, and simply being with her as her daughter or son. I doubt that, save for a rare occasion, you will have many deeply emotive or even interesting conversations with her. On the surface your visits will seem mostly routine and dry. Most times you will be talking about trivial, everyday things. "The kids are fine." "Steve dropped in last week." "Mom, your food really is bland. How can you stand all that Jell-O?" "No, we didn't get much rain, just a sprinkle." Given that you're busy and preoccupied with many pressures in your own life, it is natural that you will sneak the occasional glance at your watch.

But if you persevere in these regular visits with your mother, month after month, year after year, among everyone in the whole world, you will grow to know your mother the most deeply and she will grow to know you the most deeply. That's because at a deep level of relationship, the real connection between us takes place below the surface of our conversations. We begin to know each other through simple presence.

Prayer is the same. If we pray faithfully every day, year in and year out, we can expect little excitement, lots of boredom, and regular temptations to look at the clock. But a bond and an intimacy will be growing under the surface: a deep, growing bond with our God.

False Notions of Prayer

Why is it so difficult to pray regularly?

Some reasons are obvious: over-busyness, tiredness, and too many demands on our time. But there are other reasons too, suggested by monks and people we think of as mystics. The problem we have in sustaining prayer, they say, is often grounded in the false notion that prayer needs to be exciting, intense, and full of energy all the time.

That is impossible! Nothing is meant to be exciting all the time, including prayer and church services, and nobody has the energy to be alert, attentive, intense, and actively engaged every minute.

Like eating, prayer is meant to respect the natural rhythms of our energy. As we know from experience, we don't always want a banquet. If we tried to have a banquet every day, we would soon find coming to the table burdensome and we would look for every excuse to escape, to sneak off for a quick sandwich by ourselves. Eating has a natural balance: banquets alternate with quick snacks, rich dishes with simple sandwiches, meals that take a whole evening with meals we eat on the run. We can have high season only if we mostly have ordinary time. Healthy eating habits respect our natural rhythms: our time, energy, tiredness, the season, the hour, our taste.

Prayer should be the same, but this isn't generally respected. Too often we are left with the impression that all prayer should be high celebration, upbeat, with high energy. The more variety, the better. Longer is better than shorter. No wonder we often lack the energy to pray and want to avoid church services!

The solution is not so much new prayer forms and more variety, but rhythm, routine, and established ritual. For monks, the key to sustaining a daily life of prayer is not novelty or the call for higher energy, but rather a reliance on the expected, the familiar, the repetitious, the ritual. What's needed is a clearly delineated prayer form that does not demand of you an energy you cannot muster on a given day.

There are times, of course, for high celebration, for variety and novelty, for spontaneity, and for long ceremonies. There are also times—and these are meant to predominate just as they do in our eating habits—for ordinary time, for low season, for prayer that respects our energy level, work pressures, and time constraints.

It is no accident, I suspect, that more people used to attend daily church services when these were shorter, simpler, and less demanding in terms of energy expenditure, and gave people attending a clear expectation as to how long they would last. The same holds true for the Office of the Church and all common prayer. What clear rituals provide is prayer that depends precisely upon something beyond our own energy. The rituals carry us: our tiredness, our inattentiveness, our indifference, and even our occasional distaste. They keep us praying even when we are too tired to muster up our own energy.

False Feelings in Prayer

Prayer, as one of its oldest definitions puts it, is "lifting mind and heart to God." That sounds simple, but it is hard to do. Why?

Because we have the wrong notion of what that means. We unconsciously nurse the idea that we can pray only when we are not distracted, not angry, not emotionally or sexually preoccupied. We think God is like a parent who wants to see us only on our best behavior. So we go into God's presence only when we have nothing to hide, are joy-filled, and feel we can give proper attention to God in a reverent and loving way. Because we don't understand what prayer is, we treat God as an authority figure or a visiting dignitary—as someone to whom we don't tell the real truth. We don't tell God what is really going on in our lives. We tell God what we think God wants to hear.

Because of this, we find it difficult to pray with any regularity. What happens is we go to pray, privately or in church, feeling tired, preoccupied, perhaps even angry at someone. We bracket what we are actually feeling and instead try to crank up praise, reverence, and gratitude to God. Of course it doesn't work! Our hearts and heads (because they are preoccupied with our real issues) grow distracted.

We get the sense that what we are doing—trying to pray—is not something we can do right now and we leave it for some other time.

But the problem is not that our prayer is unreal or that the moment isn't right. The problem is that we are trying to lift to God thoughts and feelings that are not our own. If we take seriously that prayer is "lifting mind and heart to God," then every feeling and every thought we have is a valid and apt entry into prayer, no matter how irreverent, unholy, selfish, sexual, or angry that thought or feeling might seem.

Simply put, if you go to pray and you are feeling angry, pray anger; if you are sexually preoccupied, pray that preoccupation; if you are feeling murderous, pray murder; and if you are feeling full of fervor and want to praise and thank God, pray fervor. Every thought or feeling is a valid entry into prayer. What's important is that we pray what's inside of us and not what we think God would like to see inside of us.

What's so unfortunate is that, most often, because we misunderstand prayer, we stay away from it just when we most need it. We try to pray only when we feel good, centered, reverent, and worthy of praying. But we don't try to pray precisely when we most need it; that is, when we are feeling bad, irreverent, sinful, emotionally and sexually preoccupied, and unworthy of praying.

But all of these feelings can be our entry into prayer. No matter the headache or the heartache, we need only to lift it up to God.

False Expectations in Prayer

What does it mean to be holy or perfect?

There are two classical concepts of perfection, one Greek and the other Hebrew. In the Greek ideal, to be perfect is to have no deficiencies, no faults, no flaws. Perfection, to the Greek mind, means to measure up to some ideal standard, to be completely whole, true, good, and beautiful. To be perfect is never to sin.

The Hebrew ideal of perfection is quite different. In this mindset, to be perfect simply means to walk with God, despite our flaws. Perfection here means being in the divine presence, in spite of the fact that we are not perfectly whole, good, true, and beautiful.

Our concept of holiness in the West has been, both for good and bad, very much shaped by the Greek ideal of perfection. Hence, holiness has been understood as a question of measuring up to a certain benchmark. In such a view of things, a view with which many of us were raised, sanctity is understood as achieving and maintaining something—namely, moral goodness and integrity.

Such a view is not without its merits. It is a perpetual challenge against mediocrity, laziness, giving in to the line of least resistance, and settling for what is second best. Such a view of perfection (and the spirituality it engenders) keeps the ideal squarely in view. The flag is always held high, ahead of us, beckoning us, calling us beyond the limits of our present tiredness. We are always invited to something higher. This can be very healthy, especially in a culture that is cynical and despairing of ideals.

But such a concept of perfection also has a nasty underside. Nobody measures up. In the end, we all fall short, which leads to a whole series of spiritual pitfalls. First of all, we beat ourselves up with the false expectation that we can somehow, all on our own, through sheer will power, fix all that is wrong with us. Will power, as we now know, is powerless in the face of our addictions. Because we don't recognize this, we often grow discouraged and simply quit trying to break some bad habit. Why try when the result is always the same? The temptation then is to do what we in fact so often do, namely, split off holiness and project it onto to a "Mother Teresa" type of figure. We let her carry holiness for us because we believe we are unable to become holy ourselves.

Worse still, when perfection means measuring up, we find it hard to forgive ourselves and others for not being God. When the dominant idea of holiness is something that only God can measure up to, it is not easy to give others or ourselves permission to be human. We carry around a lot of discouragement, guilt, and lack of forgiveness because of this.

Hence, despite the positives that are contained in the Greek concept of perfection, we might well profit from incorporating into our lives more of the Hebrew ideal. Perfection here means walking with God, despite imperfection.

All on our own, we can never measure up. We can never be perfect in the Greek sense. But that is not what God is asking of us. What God is asking is that we bring our helplessness, weaknesses, imperfections, and sin constantly to him, that we walk with him, and that we never hide from him. God is a good parent. He understands that we will make mistakes and disappoint him and ourselves. What God asks is simply that we come home, that we share our lives with him, that we let him help us in those ways in which we are powerless to help ourselves.

Our Shame and Nakedness

Shame on you! You should know better! How often have we heard those awful words? How often have we seen them, unspoken, real, in another's eyes? Perhaps there are no words, but the message is clear: *You should be ashamed of yourself!* That's raw hurt—a whip on bare flesh!

Shame is part of life. Most of the time we connect it to a particular quality about ourselves. We are ashamed of something. Something about us is not quite right: our ignorance, our selfishness, our sexual darkness, our laziness, our loneliness, our past, our poverty, our lack of sophistication, our hidden phobia, our height, our fatness, our complexion, our hair, our birthmark, our smells, our addiction. We are all ashamed of something.

The importance of this should never be understated, not just for psychology but also for spirituality and prayer. If we are ever to become whole and spiritual—if we are to take seriously the first words that came out of the mouth of Jesus: "Change your life and believe in the good news"—then the coldness and distrust brought upon us by shame must be overcome.

Change will not be easy. Shame is powerful. Its bite is deep, the scars permanent. Although the scars of shame are permanent, they are not necessarily fatal. We are powerfully resilient, capable of living warm and trusting lives, beyond shame. But the power to live beyond shame does not lie in some easy solution. As a wise axiom has it: Not everything can be cured or fixed, though it should be named properly. This is critical in the case of shame. It must be named properly.

There is a growing body of literature today, much of it in popular psychology circles, that tries precisely to do this, to name shame properly. Unfortunately, to my mind, it often does not name it very well. It talks about cultures of shame and religions of shame and, all too quickly, lays much of the blame for shame at the feet of those who insist on duty and on those who are less liberal sexually. Duty and sexual restraint, in this view, are the culprits.

Whatever the truth of that, it misses the deeper point. We are not most deeply shamed and hurt for the first time when we are made to feel bad on account of some unfulfilled duty or because religion and culture have not given us permission to feel good about sex and our own bodies. No. Long before that, we are shamed at a deeper level. We are shamed in our enthusiasm. We are made to feel guilty, naïve, and humiliated about our very pulse for life and about our very trust of each other. Long before we are ever told that sex is bad, or that our body isn't quite right, or that we have failed in our duty somewhere, we are told we are bad because we are so trusting and enthusiastic.

Remember as a child the number of times you ran up to somebody, someone you trusted—a parent, a teacher, a friend? Completely trusting, full of life, you tried, with a nakedness you can never bring yourself to risk again, to share something you were excited about: a leaf you had found, a drawing you had made, your report card, a story you wanted to tell, a fall you had just taken, something that was very important to you. Try to recall the warmth, trust, and spontaneity of that moment. Try to bring that feeling into your prayers with God, a God who delights in you, a God who has no use for crippling shame. Jesus said: "Love each other as I have loved you" (John 15:12). The tail-end of that sentence contains the challenge. Jesus loved us by becoming vulnerable to the point of risking humiliation and rejection. We must recover our childlike trust and try to do the same.

A Conspiracy Against Interiority

Our culture is a powerful narcotic, for good and for bad. It is important that we first underline that there's partly a good side to this. A narcotic soothes and protects against brute, raw pain. Our culture has within it every kind of thing (from medicine to entertainment) to shield us from suffering. That can be good, but a narcotic also can be bad, especially when it becomes a way of escaping reality. Where our culture is particularly dangerous, I feel, is in the way it can perpetually shield us from having to face the deeper issues of life: faith, forgiveness, morality, and mortality. It can constitute, as theologian Jan Walgrave has said, "a virtual conspiracy" against the interior life by keeping us so entertained, so busy, so preoccupied, and so distracted that we lose all focus on the deeper things.

We live in a world of instant and constant communication, of mobile phones and e-mail, of iPods that contain whole libraries of music, of television packages that contain hundreds of channels, of malls and stores that are open twenty-four hours a day, of restaurants and clubs that stay open all night, of sounds that never die and lights that never go out. We can be amused, distracted, and catered to at any time.

While that has made our lives wonderfully efficient, it also has conspired against depth. The danger, as one commentator puts it, is that we are all developing permanent attention deficit disorder. We are attentive to so many things that, ultimately, we aren't attentive to anything, particularly to what is deepest inside of us.

This isn't an abstract concept! Typically our day is so full (of work, noise, pressure, rush) that when we do finally get home and have some time when we could shut down all the stimulation, we are so fatigued that what soothes us is something that functions as a narcotic: a sporting event, a game show on television, a mindless sitcom, or anything that can calm our tensions and relax us enough to sleep. It's not bad if we do this on a given night, but it is bad when we do it every night.

What happens is that we never find the space in our lives to touch what's deepest inside of us and inside of others. Given the power of our culture, we can go along like this for years until something cracks in our lives—a loved one dies, someone breaks our heart, the doctor tells us we have a terminal disease—or some other crisis suddenly renders empty all the stimulation and entertainment in the world. Then we are forced to look into our own depth, and that can be a frightening abyss if we have spent years avoiding it.

Sometimes we need a narcotic. But we have to know when it is time to unplug the television, turn off the phone, shut down the computer, silence the iPod, lay away the sports page, and resist going out for coffee with a friend, so that, for one moment at least, we are not avoiding making friends with that one part of us, the deepest part, that someday will accompany us into the sunset.

CHAPTER TWO

Hearing God's Voice in Prayer

The Voice of the Good Shepherd

W E ARE SURROUNDED by many voices. There's rarely a moment within our waking lives that someone or something isn't calling out to us and, even in our sleep, dreams and nightmares ask for our attention.

Each voice has its own particular cadence and message. Some voices invite us in, promising us life if we do this or that or buy a certain product or idea; others threaten us. Some voices beckon us toward hatred, bitterness, and anger, while others challenge us toward love, graciousness, and forgiveness. Some voices tell us they are playful and humorous, not to be taken seriously, even as others trumpet that they are urgent and weighty, the voice of non-negotiable truth, God's voice.

Within all of these: Which is the voice of God? How do we recognize God's voice among and within all of these others?

That's not easy to answer. God, as the Scriptures tell us, is the author of everything that's good, whether it bears a religious label or not. Hence, God's voice is inside of many things that are not explicitly connected to faith and religion, just as God's voice is also not in everything that masquerades as religion. But how do we discern that?

Jesus leaves us a wonderful metaphor to work with, but it's precisely only a metaphor: He tells us he is the "Good Shepherd" and his sheep will recognize his voice among all other voices. In sharing this metaphor, he is drawing upon a practice that was common among shepherds at the time: At night, for protection and companionship, shepherds would put their flocks together into a common enclosure. They would separate the sheep in the morning by using their voices. Each shepherd had trained his sheep to be attuned to his voice and his voice only. The shepherd would walk away from the enclosure calling his sheep, oftentimes by their individual names, and they would follow him. His sheep were so attuned to his voice that they would not follow another shepherd, even if that shepherd tried to trick them by imitating the voice of their real master. Each sheep recognized intimately the voice that was safeguarding her and would not follow another voice.

So too with us: Among all the voices that surround and beckon us, we need to discern the unique cadence of God's voice. And we have a number of principles that come to us from Jesus, from Scripture, and from the deep wells of our Christian tradition that can help us discern God's voice among the multitude of voices that beckon us:

The voice of God is recognized both in whispers, and in thunder and in storm.

The voice of God is recognized in the call to what's higher and invites us to holiness, even as it is recognized in the call to humility.

The voice of God is the one that most challenges and stretches us, even as it is the only voice that ultimately soothes and comforts us.

The voice of God is always heard in a privileged way in the poor, even as it beckons us through the voice of the artist and the intellectual.

The voice of God always invites us to live beyond all fear, even as it inspires holy fear.

The voice of God is always heard wherever there is genuine enjoyment and gratitude, even as it asks us to deny ourselves and die to ourselves.

The voice of God, it would seem, is found in paradox, but it is the voice of someone who knows us intimately and calls each of us by name.

God's Acceptance and Delight

I don't often remember my dreams, nor do I put much stock in them, but, several years ago, I had a dream that caused me to do both. It highlights the most important of all truths: that God is love and that only by letting that kind of love into our lives can we save ourselves from disappointment, shame, and sadness. It went something like this:

For whatever reason, and dreams don't give you a reason, I was asked to go to an airport and pick up Jesus, who was arriving on a flight. I was understandably nervous and frightened. A bevy of apprehensions beset me: How would I recognize him? What would he look like? How would he react to me? What would I say to him? Would I like what I saw? More frightening yet, would he like what he saw when he looked at me?

With those feelings surging through me, I stood, as one stands in a dream, at the end of a long corridor nervously surveying the passengers who were walking toward me. How would I recognize Jesus, and would his first glance at me reflect his disappointment?

But this was a good dream and it taught me as much about God as I'd learned in all my years of studying theology. All of my fears were alleviated in a second. What happened was the opposite of all my expectations: Suddenly, walking down the corridor toward me was Jesus, smiling, beaming with delight, coming straight for me, rushing, eager to meet me. Everything about him was stunningly and wonderfully disarming. There was no awkward moment; everything about him erased that. His eyes, his face, and his body embraced me without reserve and without judgment. I knew he saw straight through me, knew all my faults and weaknesses, my lack of substance, and none of it mattered. And, for that moment, none of it mattered to me either. Jesus was eager to meet me!

In a moment like this, one forgets everything, except that God is here. There's no place for fear or shame or wondering what God thinks of you. That's a lesson all of us must somehow learn, somehow experience. We live with too much fear of God. Partly it is bad theology, but mostly we fear God because we've never experienced the kind of love that is manifest in God. We take for granted that anyone who sees us as we really are (in our unloveliness, weaknesses, pathology, sin, insubstantiality) will, in the end, be as disappointed with us as we are with ourselves.

At the end of the day, we expect that God is disappointed with us and will greet us with a frown. The tragedy and sadness here is that we avoid God when we are most in need of love and acceptance. Because we think God is disappointed in us, especially at those times when we are disappointed in ourselves, we fail to meet the one person, the one love, and the one energy—God—that actually understands us, accepts us, delights in us, and is eager to smile at us.

God's Unconditional Love

Experiencing the unconditional love of God is what prayer, in the end, is all about. This was brought home to me, powerfully, several years ago. A man in his mid-thirties came to see me. He didn't ask for confession, but he made one. He sat himself down and said simply: "Father, I want to tell you a story. The worst thing that could possibly happen to anyone has happened to me, and the best thing that could ever happen to anyone has also happened to me. I have been to hell and back, and being in hell led me to believe in heaven." Tears flowed freely as he told me the story:

He was a married man with three children. His marriage was basically a good one, though he had been unfaithful. Unthinking, without prayer in his life, seduced by his own selfishness and the pressures of our culture, he had drifted into a sexual affair with one of the secretaries in his office. Initially, he experienced very little guilt about the affair and continued on with his family, the Church, and his work as before. "It was incredible," he confessed, "but I was able to continue this with basically no guilt feelings whatever. In fact, I even believed that this was helping the girl involved and was making me a better husband and father."

Eventually, the girl became pregnant. Even then his irresponsibility did not sink in. He continued as before. But she didn't. Returning from a vacation with his family, he found a letter waiting for him: the girl had written to tell him that she had had an abortion, had quit her job, and had moved to another city. It was over. It was then that the reality of his sin sunk in, deeply and painfully. Before that moment, he had felt little guilt. Now, in an instant, he was overwhelmed by it. His world shattered. Guilt overcame him and, unable to see how he would ever again face God, his family, and himself, he decided, though in a vague sort of way, to kill himself.

With no particular plan in mind, he sat in his car, on the very night on which he had received the letter, and began to drive. Eventually, after some hours, he found himself on dirt roads and finally, not knowing where he was, he ran out of gas. Leaving his car, he saw an old, dilapidated church. Its doors were torn off their hinges and he walked, blindly, into the church. He fell asleep and awoke just as the sun was rising. When he looked around, he saw that the only thing left in the church was a crucifix on the front wall.

He said: "You know, Father, I'm a cradle Catholic. I've seen crucifixes all my life. But, before that moment, I had never really seen one. I looked at that cross and I understood. I had been to hell and God had never stopped loving me, even for one second!" Then he added: "I'm not proud of what I did. That sin will always be part of my past, nothing will ever erase that. But because of what I experienced in seeing that cross and knowing what it means, I can live beyond it. I know now that God loves me even when I am twisted and sinful. From that, I draw strength to live, beyond my sin."

The darkness of our personal hells, perhaps more so than anything else, can help us understand the love that makes for heaven. It's this love that we seek in prayer. The love of God is not something to be admired; it is something to be seized and lived under.

Safely in God's Hands

In Scripture, the opposite of faith is not doubt but anxiety. To lack faith is not so much to have theoretical doubts about God's existence as it is to be anxious and fearful at a deep level.

How is this possible? We cannot help but be full of anxiety and worry about many things—our loved ones, our health, our work, our future. "Will I pass this examination?" "Will my son come home this evening?" "Will my medical check-up be okay?" "Will this person reject me?" "Will I lose my job?" "Will I get this promotion?" "Can I pay my mortgage?" "Are my daughter's new friends good for her?" "Is my spouse being truthful?" "Do people like me?" "Are my clothes right?" "Will I be stuck in traffic and miss my appointment?" There is rarely a moment in our lives that is not clouded by a worry of some kind or other. We are always somewhat anxious.

Is worrying about so many things bad for our faith? Not necessarily. What opposes faith is not so much worry about this or that particular thing as worry that God has forgotten us, worry that our names are not written in heaven, that we aren't in good hands, that our lives aren't safe, and that there is every reason to fear and be anxious because, at the core of things, there isn't a benevolent, all-powerful goodness who is concerned about us.

Have you ever had the experience of going to your closet and noticing an item of clothing that you had forgotten you still possessed? You see a shirt or a blouse that you haven't worn for a long time and you say to yourself: "I still have this! I had completely forgotten about it!" It had simply slipped off your radar screen. Such a scenario is what haunts faith, the fear that we have slipped off God's radar screen, that we have been forgotten, that God will look down on earth sometime and realize with a start that we are still here: "My God, she's still there. I had completely forgotten about her!" It is this kind of anxiety, the deep fear that we have been forgotten, that pushes many of us to make an assertion of our lives. Nobody wants to live and die unnoticed, insignificant, forgotten. We are always somewhat anxious about that. This anxiety is the opposite of faith. It is not so much the fear that God doesn't exist, as the fear that God does not notice our existence.

What is faith? Faith doesn't have you believe that you will have no worries, or that you will not make mistakes, or that you and your loved ones won't sometimes fall victim to accident or sickness. What faith gives you is the assurance that God is good, that God can be trusted, that God won't forget you, and that, despite any indication to the contrary, God is still solidly in charge of this universe. Faith says that God is real and God is Lord and, because of this, there is ultimately nothing to fear. We are in safe hands. Reality is gracious, forgiving, loving, redeeming, and absolutely trustworthy. Our task is to surrender to that.

"Lord, Teach Us to Pray"

One of the places we can turn to for help in learning how to pray is the Gospel of Luke. More so than any of the other Gospels, his is the Gospel of prayer. Luke gives us glimpses of Jesus praying in virtually every kind of situation: Jesus prays when he is joy-filled, he prays when he is in agony, he prays with others around him, and he prays when he is alone at night, withdrawn from all human contact. He prays high on a mountain, on a sacred place, and he prays on the level plane, where ordinary life happens. In Luke's Gospel, Jesus prays a lot.

And the lesson isn't lost on his disciples. They sense that Jesus's real depth and power are drawn from his prayer. They know that what makes him so special, so unlike any other religious figure, is that he is linked at some deep place to a power outside of this world. And they want this for themselves. That's why they approach Jesus and ask him: "Lord, teach us to pray!"

But we must be careful not to misunderstand what constituted their attraction and what they were asking for when they asked Jesus to teach them how to pray. They sensed that what Jesus drew from the depth of his prayer was not, first of all, his power to do miracles or to silence his enemies with some kind of superior intelligence. What impressed them and what they wanted for their own lives was the depth and graciousness of his soul. The power they admired and wanted was Jesus's power to love and forgive his enemies rather than embarrass and crush them. What they wanted was Jesus's power to transform a room, not by some miraculous deed, but by a disarming innocence and vulnerability that, like a baby's presence, has everyone solicitously guarding his or her behavior and language. What they wanted was his power to renounce life in self-sacrifice, even while retaining the enviable capacity to enjoy the pleasures of life without guilt. What they wanted was Jesus's power to be big-hearted, to love beyond his own tribe, to love poor and rich alike, to live inside of charity, joy, peace, patience, goodness, long-suffering, fidelity, mildness, and chastity, despite everything within life that militates against these virtues.

The disciples recognized that this power did not come from within Jesus, but from a source outside him. They saw that he connected to a deep source through prayer, through constantly lifting to God what was on his mind and in his heart. They saw it and they wanted that depth-connection for themselves. So they asked Jesus to teach them how to pray.

Ultimately, we too want Jesus's depth and graciousness in our own lives. Like Jesus's disciples, we also know we can attain this only through prayer, through accessing a power that lies inside the deepest deep of our souls and beyond our souls. We know too that the route to that depth lies in journeying inward, in silence, through both the pain and the quiet, the chaos and the peace, that come to us when we still ourselves to pray.

Searching for Solitude

Our lives are often like over-packed suitcases. It seems we are always busy, always over-pressured, always one phone call, one text message, one e-mail, one visit, and one task behind. We are forever anxious about what we have left undone, about whom we have disappointed, about unmet expectations.

Inside of all of that, we have no quiet island to escape to, no haven of solitude. We can always be reached. Half the world has our contact numbers and we feel pressure to be available all the time. So we often feel as if we are on a treadmill from which we want to step off. And within all that busyness, pressure, noise, and tiredness we long for solitude, long for some quiet, peaceful refuge where all the pressure and noise will stop and we can sit in simple rest. That's a healthy yearning. It's our soul speaking. Like our bodies, our souls keep trying to tell us what they need. They need solitude, but solitude isn't easy to find.

Let me share a personal experience:

Several years ago, when I was teaching theology at a college, I made arrangements to spend two months in summer living at a Trappist monastery. I was seeking solitude, seeking to slow down my life. I had just finished a very pressured semester, teaching, doing formation work, giving talks and workshops, and trying to do some writing. I had a near-delicious fantasy of what was to meet me at the monastery. I would have two wonderful months of solitude: I would light the fireplace in the guesthouse and sit quietly by it. I would take a quiet walk in the woods behind the monastery. I would sit on an outdoor rocking chair by a little lake on the property and smoke my pipe. I would enjoy wholesome food, eating in silence as I listened to a monk reading aloud from a spiritual book, and, best of all, I would join the monks for their prayers—singing the Office in choir, celebrating the Eucharist, and sitting in quiet meditation with them in their "stillness chapel."

I arrived at the monastery mid-afternoon, hastily unpacked, and set about immediately doing these things. By late evening I had mowed them all down, like a lawn that had been waiting to be cut. I had lit the fire and sat by it. I had taken a walk in the woods, smoked my pipe on the rocking chair by the lake, joined the monks in choir for vespers, sat in meditation with them afterward for half an hour, eaten a wholesome supper in silence, and then joined them again for sung Compline. By bedtime the first evening, I already had done all the things I had fantasized would bring me solitude and I went to bed restless, anxious about how I would survive the next two months without television, newspapers, phone calls, socializing with friends, and my regular work to distract me. I had done all the right solitude activities and had not found solitude, but had found restlessness instead. It took several weeks before my body and mind slowed down enough for me to find a basic restfulness, before I could even begin to nibble at the edges of solitude.

Solitude is not something we turn on like a water faucet. It needs a body and mind slowed enough to be attentive to the present moment. We are in solitude when, as Thomas Merton describes it, we fully taste the water we are drinking, feel the warmth of our blankets, and are restful enough to be content inside our own skin.

We don't often accomplish this, despite sincere effort. But we need to keep making new beginnings.

CHAPTER THREE

Understanding Priestly Prayer

A Symphony of Prayer

THEOLOGIANS MAKE AN important distinction between what they call "devotional" and "liturgical" prayer. Devotional prayer, they tell us, is private in nature and is meant to help sustain us personally on the spiritual journey. Liturgical prayer, by contrast, is public by nature, is the Church's prayer (not our own), is universal in scope, and is intended for the needs of the world.

Perhaps we might understand this better if we put different names to these. What helps clarify things for me are the terms "affective" and "priestly" prayer. "Affective" prayer refers to private prayer, prayer that's about us, focused precisely on bringing us and our feelings to God. "Priestly" prayer, on the other hand, is not about us; it is about the world and for the world.

Unfortunately, we often confuse these two kinds of prayer. For example, five hundred people might be sitting in meditation together in a church or praying the rosary together at a shrine and this is still private or devotional prayer. Conversely, someone might be praying the Office of the Church alone at home in an armchair, or a priest might be celebrating the Eucharist alone at a kitchen table, and this is still public, liturgical prayer. The distinction, as we see from these examples, is not dependent upon the number of people participating, or whether the prayer is taking place in a church, or even whether the prayer is being prayed in a group or privately.

What is priestly prayer, then? Priestly prayer is the prayer of Christ through the Church for the world. Our Christian belief is that Christ is still gathering us together around his Word and is still offering an eternal act of love for the world. As an extension of that, we believe that whenever we meet together, in a church or elsewhere, to gather around the Scriptures or to celebrate the Eucharist, we are entering into that prayer and sacrifice of Christ. This is liturgical prayer, and it is Christ's prayer, not ours. We also pray liturgically whenever we pray, in community or privately, something called the Office of the Church.

This kind of prayer is not restricted to the ordained clergy. We are all priests by virtue of our baptism, and part of the implicit covenant we make with the community at our baptism is the commitment, when we reach adulthood, to pray habitually for the world through the liturgical prayer of the Church.

What needs also to be highlighted here, because we easily miss this aspect, is that the Church's liturgical prayer is for the world, not for itself. The Church does not exist for its own sake, but as an instrument of salvation for the world. Its function is to save the world, not itself. In liturgical prayer we pray with Christ, through the Church, but for the world.

An analogy might be helpful: Imagine you're part of a symphony orchestra, playing an instrument that contributes to an overall musical score. Night in and night out, you're playing the same piece in the same theater, helping to create a beautiful symphony for the audience. The public prayer of the Church, priestly prayer, works exactly like that: it makes a symphony of prayer for the benefit of everyone.

The Divine Office

The Divine Office (also called the "Breviary" or the "Liturgy of the Hours") is available daily as the priestly prayer for those who are not ordained ministers in the Church. This is especially true for two of those liturgical hours, Lauds (Morning Prayer) and Vespers (Evening Prayer). They, unlike the other hours, which are more the particular domain of monks and professional contemplatives, are the ordinary priestly prayer of the laity. Unlike private prayer and contemplation, in which we should change methods whenever praying becomes dry or sterile, Lauds and Vespers are prayers of the universal Church that are in essence intended to be communal and priestly. They don't have to be relevant for our private lives. We pray them as elders, as baptized adults, as priests, to invoke God's blessing upon the world.

Whenever we pray Lauds or Vespers, we take on a universal voice. We are no longer just a private individual praying: we are the voice, body, and soul of the earth itself, continuing the high priesthood of Christ, offering prayers and entreaties, aloud and in silent tears, to God for the sake of the world.

We pray as a microcosm of the whole world, even as we pray for the whole world. In essence, we are saying this:

Lord, God, I stand before you as a microcosm of the earth itself, to give it voice: See in my openness, the world's openness; in my infidelity, the world's infidelity; in my sincerity, the world's sincerity; in my hypocrisy, the world's hypocrisy; in my generosity, the world's generosity; in my selfishness, the world's selfishness; in my attentiveness, the world's attentiveness; in my distraction, the world's distraction; in my desire to praise you, the world's desire to praise you; and in my self-preoccupation, the world's forgetfulness of you.

For I am of the earth, a piece of earth, and the earth opens or closes to you through my body, my soul, and my voice. I am your priest on earth.

And what I hold up for you today is all that is in this world, both of joy and of suffering. I offer you the bread of the world's achievements, even as I offer you the wine of its failure, the blood of all that's crushed as those achievements take place. I offer you the powerful of our world, our rich, our famous, our athletes, our artists, our movie stars, our entrepreneurs, our young, our healthy, and everything that's creative and bursting with life, even as I offer you those who are weak, feeble, aged, crushed, sick, dying, and victimized. I offer to you all the pagan beauties, pleasures, and joys of this life, even as I stand with you under the cross, affirming that the one who is excluded from earthly pleasure is the cornerstone of the community. I offer you the strong and arrogant, along with the weak and gentle of heart, asking you to bless both and to stretch my heart so that it can, like you, hold and bless everything that is. I offer you both the wonders and the pains of this world, your world.

Our Need to Celebrate

Why do we need to celebrate? What causes that urge in us? We have a deep need to celebrate because certain moments and events of our lives (e.g., a birthday, a wedding, a graduation, a commitment, an achievement) demand that they be celebrated. They demand that we surround them with rituals, which heighten and intensify their meaning and link us to others.

The same is true of many of our deep erotic, playful, and creative feelings. They demand to be celebrated: shared, heightened, widened, and linked to others. Ultimately we have a need for ecstasy (from the Latin *ex stasis*, which means to stand outside of ourselves in heightened self-awareness). But given our guilt complexes and our inhibitions, we often make pseudo-celebration.

What do most of us do when we celebrate? We overdo. We take a lot of things we ordinarily do—drinking, eating, loving, talking, singing, humoring, and so on—and we simply take them to excess. We eat too much, drink too much, sing too loudly, tell one joke too many, simulate love too often.

We try to attain ecstasy by pushing ourselves beyond our normal senses. But for all our frenzied attempts, there is precious little genuine enjoyment. Occasionally, we do succeed and we genuinely celebrate: we join others and feel ourselves being widened and made larger, in community, in playfulness, in love. But that happens seldom, and never in frenzy. Mostly the party is followed by a hangover, either physical, emotional, or psychological. The reasons for this are complex, deep, and too often hidden from us. I would like to try to flesh out one of them.

The main reason we find it so difficult to truly celebrate is that we lack the capacity to genuinely enjoy, to simply take life, pleasure, and love as a gift from God, pure and simple. Perhaps I shouldn't say we lack this capacity, because we have it as a God-given gift. More correctly, our capacity to enjoy too often is buried under a mound of what psychologists would call collective neurotic guilt. That is a heavy term, but it means simply that too often we cannot enjoy what is legitimate and given us by God to enjoy because somehow, consciously or unconsciously, we sense that all of our pleasures are "stealing from God." This feeling wounds most of us. Somehow, in the name of God, we deprive ourselves of the right to enjoy.

Too often this leads to a dangerous confusion: we begin to confuse pleasure with enjoyment, excess with ecstasy, and the denial of self-consciousness with the heightened awareness that community brings. All the unfulfilling substitutes in the world won't fill what's missing because we haven't celebrated.

Christ came and declared a wedding feast, a celebration, at the very center of life. They crucified him not for being too ascetical, but because he told us that we might enjoy life. He told us that life will give us more goodness and enjoyment than we can stand, if we can learn to receive it without fear. But we are still in exile, without wedding garments, looking for the key to the room of celebration. Perhaps we need to be just a bit more earnest and sincere when we say the words, "your kingdom come!"

Good Liturgy: The Role of the Celebrant

Perhaps the most frequent complaint one hears in church circles is that our liturgical gatherings are boring. Usually the celebrant, the priest, is singled out as the culprit who is responsible and is asked to bear the brunt of the criticism. He is accused of being dead, uninspiring, bland, and a poor preacher. As a priest, I take more than a casual offense to this critique. It is not that I deny its truth. Heaven knows, most of the time our celebrations are dull.

But the fault, when there is one, is not solely ours as priests. In fact, often there is no fault whatever, save the unrealistic expectations of those attending the celebration. Are liturgical gatherings always meant to be enthusiastic, bouncy celebrations? Is the celebrant responsible for making the celebration exciting?

The answers to those questions are not so obvious. Good liturgy is good psychology. It flows with the psychological rhythms of those who are attending. As we've said, good prayer means "lifting mind and heart to God." Given that, the issue grows very complex.

Our psyches go up and down. We have our seasons and days of joyfulness. Sometimes we feel like singing and dancing. Sometimes there is spring in our step. But we have other seasons, too—cold seasons, bland seasons, seasons of tiredness, pain, illness, and boredom. If prayer is lifting heart and mind to God, then clearly during those times we should be lifting something other than song and dance.

The celebrant's role is to help gather everything together and direct it upward, like incense smoke to God. Thus, the best celebrant is not necessarily the one who conducts the most enthusiastic celebration, nor even the one who delivers the best homily. Sometimes the celebrant's very efforts to do this can do violence to the persons who are attending.

The best celebrant is the person who can act as a radar screen, lifting up not just the bread and wine, but all that the people bring, including their tiredness, their hangovers, their woundedness, their emotional and sexual preoccupations, and their boredom. The celebrant gathers it all together and offers it as it is, not as he would like it to be.

There is a story told about a Jewish farmer who did not get home before sunset one Sabbath and was forced to spend the night in the field, waiting for sunrise the next day before being able to return home. Upon his return home he was met by a rather perturbed rabbi who chided him for his carelessness. "What did you do out there all night in the field?" the rabbi asked him. "Did you at least pray?" The farmer answered: "Rabbi, I am not a clever man. I don't know how to pray properly. What I did was to simply recite the alphabet all night and let God form the words for himself."

When we come to celebrate, we bring the alphabet of our lives. If our hearts and minds are full of warmth, love, enthusiasm, song, and dance, then these are the letters we bring. If they are full of tiredness, despair, blandness, pain, and boredom, then those are our letters. Bring them. Spend them. Celebrate them. Offer them. It is God's task to make the words!

Good Liturgy: Our Role

Part of our Christian faith, as canonized in our creed, is the belief that our unity and community with each other in Christ is so real, so deep, so physical, and so mutually interdependent that we constitute not an aggregate or a corporation but an organism, a living body. The body of Christ is not a body in the way General Motors is a body, but it is a body in the way that a man or woman is a body. The unity inside that body is not mystical or analogical, it's real.

Thus, Christ taught, and the saints believed, that the most private spiritual and moral battles that go on inside one's conscience have an effect for good or for bad on all of humanity. Just as in any physical body there are visible aspects that can be observed with the naked eye and other invisible aspects that go on under the surface and escape simple observation, so it is within the body of Christ. Most of what is happening regarding health or disease within the body is, long before it shows up externally, not observable to the unaided eye. Enzymes, bacteria, viruses, and antibodies do their work for health or disease invisibly. By the time we see external symptoms, they already have been working for a long time.

This is also true inside the body of Christ. The things that, in the end, preserve health or cause disease are, like viruses and antibodies, invisible. They are seen only in their eventual effect on the body. What happens for health or for disease in any one cell, be it ever so small, eventually affects the health of the whole body. This idea, of course, can be badly understood. But in an age that de-emphasizes private morality, we tend to forget that a body needs a strong immune system and healthy antibodies to keep it free of disease.

What are the antibodies that create a healthy immune system within the body of Christ? If we can believe those who have been doctors of the soul, we create healthy antibodies when we silently suffer for each other, when we pray for each other, when we live out lives of quiet martyrdom, and when we emerge victorious in our little battles with what's petty inside of us. Our seemingly small sins—the grudge, the little lie, and the petty jealousy—do make a difference.

God cares about the little things as much as he cares about the great ones. God cares because the little things shape the big things. Social morality is simply a reflection of private morality. The global picture is what the microcosm of the human heart looks like when it is magnified.

When the chaos that lies within the recesses of our private lives remains untouched and untamed, it will remain untouched and untamable in the world at large. The kingdom of God works by conversion, and conversion, in the final analysis, is an eminently personal act. Carlos Castañeda, the Peruvian-American mystic, says: "I came from Latin America where intellectuals were always talking about political and social revolution and where a lot of bombs were thrown. But revolution hasn't changed much. It takes little daring to bomb a building, but in order to give up cigarettes or to stop being anxious or to stop internal chattering, you have to remake yourself. This is where real reform begins."

CHAPTER FOUR

Practicing Affective Prayer

The Aim of Affective Prayer

P RIVATE OR "AFFECTIVE" prayer has many forms—meditation, centering prayer, praying the rosary, and devotional prayers of all kinds. But affective prayer has a single aim: to draw us and our loved ones into deeper intimacy with Christ.

In the end, no matter its particular form, and even when it is done publicly or in a large group, all private and devotional prayer can be defined in this way: it is prayer that tries, in myriad ways, to open us up in such a way that we can hear God say to us, "I love you!"

A story might help here. A number of years ago, I attended a weeklong retreat given by Bob Michel, an Oblate colleague and a highly sought-after spiritual mentor. His approach was disarming. Most of us are forever looking for something novel, at the cutting edge, outside the box, something complex. But what he offered was stunningly simple and down-to-earth. He spent the whole time trying to teach us how to pray in an affective way. In essence, what he told us might be summarized this way: *You must try to pray so that, in your prayer, you open yourself in such a way that sometime—perhaps not today, but sometime—you are able to hear God say to you, "I love you!" These words, addressed to you by God, are the most important words you will ever hear because, before you hear them, nothing is ever completely right with you, but after you hear them, something will be right in your life at a very deep level.*

This might sound pious and sentimental. It is anything but that. Do not be put off by simplicity. The simpler something is, the harder it is to wrap our minds around it. That is true of prayer. It's so simple that we rarely lay bare its essence.

John's Gospel already makes that point. The Gospel of John structures itself very differently from the other Gospels. John has no infancy narratives or early life of Jesus. In his Gospel, we meet Jesus as an adult right on the first page, and the first words out of Jesus's mouth are a question: "What are you looking for?" That question remains throughout the rest of the Gospel as an undergirding, suggesting that beneath everything else a certain search is forever going on. A lot of things are happening on the surface, but underneath, there remains always the nagging, restless question: "What are you looking for?"

Jesus answers that question explicitly only at the end of the Gospel, on the morning of the resurrection. Mary Magdalene goes looking for him, carrying spices with which to embalm his dead body. Jesus meets her, alive and in no need of embalming, but she doesn't recognize him. Bewildered but sincere, she asks Jesus where she might find him. Jesus repeats for her the question with which he opened the Gospel: "What are you looking for?" Then he answers it. With deep affection, Jesus pronounces her name: "Mary." In the end, that's what we are all looking for and most need. We need to hear God, affectionately, one to one, saying our name. "Carolyn!" "Tom!" "Maria!" "Joseph!"

Moreover, because prayer is meant to be a mutual thing, it is important that we respond in kind. Part of affective prayer is that we, too, one to one, with affection, at least occasionally say the same thing to God: "I love you!" In all long-term, affectionate relationships, the partners occasionally have to prompt each other to hear expressions of affection and reassurance. The relationship of prayer is no different.

Being Bold in Prayer

The classic definition of prayer tells us that prayer is raising mind and heart to God. In essence, that says it all. The problem is that we often raise our minds but not our hearts. Our prayer tends to be intellectual but not affective, and we tend to think of prayer more as a way of gaining insight than as a way of being touched in the heart.

But ultimately, prayer is about love, not insight. It is meant to establish friendship. Friendship, as we know, is not as much a question of having insight into each other's lives as it is of mutually touching each other in affection and understanding. Friendship, as John of the Cross puts it, is a question of attaining "boldness with each other." When we have touched each other's lives deeply, we can be bold with each other. We can then ask each other for help, ask each other to be present without needing an excuse, or share our deepest feelings. Good friendship inspires boldness.

The object of prayer is precisely to try to attain this kind of "boldness" with God, to try to reach a point where we are comfortable enough with God to ask for help, just as we would a trusted friend. But to reach this kind of trust we first must let God touch us in the heart, and not just in insight. This means prayer is not so much a question of having beautiful thoughts about God as it is of feeling God's affection for us. Sadly, that is what we generally miss in prayer: the experience of God's affection.

What is common in prayer is the tendency to talk to ourselves rather than to God. For example: When we are at prayer and we begin to have various feelings and insights, the almost automatic reaction is to begin to speak to ourselves about what's happening in us, saying things like: "This is wonderful!" "This scares me!" "I shouldn't be feeling this way!" "I can't wait to write this down!" When this happens, we end up speaking to ourselves rather than to God.

This point was clarified for me recently on a retreat. The retreat director suggested that perhaps the number-one problem in prayer, among those who seriously try to sustain private prayer, is the tendency to constantly talk to ourselves, not to God. As the director said, "There are persons who adore themselves before the Blessed Sacrament." He suggested that too often in prayer we say things to ourselves that we should be saying to God. The key to prayer, in his view, is to turn from ourselves to God.

And the pivotal part of that turning is that we must ask God to touch us affectively and not just intellectually. When we go to pray, what we most need to ask for is to hear God's voice within us saying: "I love you!" Nothing will heal us more and nothing will make us more bold before life's mystery and goodness than hearing those words from God. Our very capacity to love depends upon it.

Prayer as Surrender

It's not easy to be centered, rooted, secure in who we are, able to give the world our best. More commonly, we find ourselves adrift, unsure of ourselves, with most of what's best in us still frustrated, buried, waiting for a better day. Too many things, it seems, conspire against us living out what's truest and best inside us.

We'd like to be grounded, be ourselves, have a clear direction in life, be free of compulsions, and live out more our dignity, goodness, and creativity; but too many things push us the opposite way. Ideology, anger, bitterness, envy, restlessness, confusion, moral compromise, and the simple need to get by all pull us down. We end up giving into various compensations (as substitutes for what we really want) and thus we quietly despair of ever embracing our dignity, talents, and solitude at any high level.

Why does it happen? It happens because we cannot stay steady in a churning sea without a good anchor, we cannot avoid giving into compensation unless what's highest in us is given enough expression, and we cannot deal with the issues of finitude unless we have some transcendent focus. Unless we are anchored in something beyond the here and now, chances are we will drown in the present moment.

Jesus models the kind of prayer we need to cope with a world that goes mad at times, and with hearts prone to drink in that madness. The Gospels describe Jesus praying in different ways, but sometimes they simply say, "He turned his eyes toward heaven!" The same expression is used of other great faith figures—Stephen, Paul, the early martyrs—and it's used of them precisely at those times when the forces of madness are threatening to kill them. When the world around them is going mad, they "turn their eyes toward heaven."

What made Jesus different (and what makes any prayerful person different) is not superior will power, less-fiery emotions, monastic withdrawal from the temptations of the world, or intellectual insight. Prayer is not a question of insight, of being smarter than anyone else; nor of will, of being stronger than anyone else; nor of emotional restraint or sexual aloofness, of being less passionate than anyone else; nor of withdrawal, of being less exposed to temptation than anyone else. Prayer is a question of unity and surrender—of uniting one's will with someone else and surrendering one's will to that other. Prayer is the desire to be in union with someone, especially in union with that other's will.

Perhaps the people who have understood this best are Alcoholics Anonymous groups. They realized long ago that it's not by strength of will or by intellectual insight that we keep from drowning. Nobody with an addiction of any kind has ever studied or willed their way out of that. Through pain and humiliation, he or she has come to realize there is only one way out of helplessness: surrender of one's will to a higher power, to God. In essence, people get together at twelve-step meetings to "turn their eyes toward heaven."

Each of us needs to find our own way of doing this if we are to cope with the forces that threaten to drown us. It's not through study or will power that we will rise above our moral ineptitude, the endless practical demands of life, and the compensations we give into to cope. We will always be adrift, until we, like Jesus, regularly "turn our eyes toward heaven." In my experience, the extraordinary people I have known and admired all have had the same secret: they prayed privately.

Contemplative Prayer

One of the great spiritual writers of our time was Thomas Merton, a Trappist monk. Merton, though, wasn't born in a monastery. A checkered past and a driving restlessness led him there, and what he was looking for was solitude, respite from a temperament that would not let him rest.

His mother and father had been artists, and Merton inherited from them those qualities that make for a good artist: huge talent, a fertile imagination, and a punishing restlessness. By the time he was twenty-five he was poised professionally to do great things, but his personal life was a mess. More than that, he was dying, literally, because he couldn't slow down, anchor himself in everyday life, and simply rest. Restlessness was beating him up like a playground bully. He wasn't eating properly or sleeping regularly, and he had no redeeming rhythm or routine to his life. He was spending his nights in jazz clubs, living on cigarettes and alcohol, and nursing a stomach ulcer. His health was deteriorating dangerously. Spiritually and morally, he was searching, sincerely and even desperately, for someone or something to commit himself to, but even as he flirted with faith and Church, his restlessness and bad habits made it difficult for him to commit to anything in a consistent way. There's an infamous story told of how he used to hang around Catherine Doherty's early Madonna House community in New York, until Catherine one day told him to stay away because he was a bad influence.

His honesty eventually paid off and Merton took the plunge of faith. Leaving New York, career, and friends behind, he entered the Trappist Abbey in Kentucky. He did it, in his own words, to save his life, having realized that, unless he did something as radical as this, he would die soon. He did it, too, to search for God and to find something that had eluded him all his life: simple rest.

Initially, the monastery did for him what he had hoped for; it gave him a sense of God's presence, a clear direction in life, and a calm body and spirit. He went through a burst of first-fervor that he shared with the world in his classic autobiography, *The Seven Storey Mountain*. But restlessness, as we know, cannot be turned on and off like a water tap. It seeps through even monastery doors. Merton's restlessness returned, but now, as a monk, Merton had an answer for it. His answer? Contemplative prayer, solitude.

Contemplative prayer is the answer to restlessness. But Merton learned that it is not an easy thing, not a technique you master at a weekend seminar. During the last years of his life, living as a hermit, he tried to explore more deeply what it meant to live in solitude and contemplation. What he eventually learned and recorded in his diaries during those years surprised him. Contemplation, he found out, is not some altered form of consciousness, nor a blank consciousness emptied of all thought and feeling, nor even a consciousness that empties itself of everything except thoughts and feelings about God. And solitude, he came to realize, is not something we attain once and for all. We don't divide our lives into "before" and "after" we have found solitude. Rather, our hours and our days are divided between those times when we are more in solitude and those times when we are more caught up in the distractions of our work and the heartaches of our restlessness.

Contemplation is not, first and foremost, a technique for prayer. Sometimes prayer, especially centering prayer, can help us find it, but contemplation is something more. It's a way of being present to what's really inside our own experience. We are in solitude, in contemplation, in prayer, when we feel the warmth of a blanket, taste the flavor of coffee, share love and friendship, and perform the everyday tasks of our lives so as to perceive in them that our lives aren't little or anonymous or unimportant, but that what's timeless and eternal is in the ordinary of our lives.

Dogged Fidelity

Several years ago, a friend shared this story with me: Raised a Roman Catholic and essentially faithful in going to church and in trying to live an honest, moral life, he found himself, in his mid-forties, plagued by doubts about God and unable to pray.

Anxious about this and looking for spiritual guidance, he went to see a Jesuit priest who had a reputation as a spiritual director. The advice he received sounded so simplistic, it triggered irritation rather than hope. The Jesuit said: "Make a promise to yourself to sit in silent prayer for a half an hour a day for the next six months. If you are faithful to that, you will recover your sense of God." My friend protested, but the Jesuit persisted: "Just do it! Show up and sit in silent prayer, even if you feel like you are talking to a wall. It's the only practical advice I can give you." Despite his skepticism, my friend took the Jesuit's advice and, six months later, his sense of God indeed had returned.

This story highlights something important: our sense of God's existence is very much linked to fidelity to prayer. However—and this is the Catch-22—we struggle to sustain long-term, real prayer in our lives.

Prayer is easy only for beginners and for those who are already saints. During all the long years in between, it is difficult. Why? Because prayer has the same inner dynamics as love, and love is sweet only in its initial stage, when we first fall in love, and again in its final, mature stage. In between, love is hard work, dogged fidelity, and needs willful commitment beyond what is normally provided by our emotions and our imagination.

Prayer works in the same way. As we grow deeper and more mature in our relationship to God, just as in a relationship to someone we love, reality begins to dispel an illusion. It's not that we become disillusioned with God, but rather that we come to realize that so many of the warm thoughts and feelings we believed were about God were really about ourselves. Disillusionment is a good thing. It's the dispelling of an illusion. What we thought was prayer was partly a spell of enchantment about ourselves. When that disillusionment sets in—and this a maturing moment in our lives—it is easy to believe that we were deluded about the other, the person we had fallen in love with or, in the case of prayer, God. The easy response then is to back away, to quit, to see the whole thing as having been an illusion, a false start. In the spiritual life, that's usually when we stop praying. The opposite is called for. What we need to do then is to show up, just as we did before, minus the warm thoughts and feelings: bored, uncertain, and stripped of our enchantment about ourselves. The deeper we go in relationships and in prayer, the more unsure of ourselves we become, and this is the beginning of maturity.

It's when I say, "I don't know how to love," and, "I don't know how to pray," that I first begin to understand what love and prayer actually are.

The Domestic Monastery

There is a tradition, strong among spiritual writers, that we will not advance within the spiritual life unless we pray at least an hour a day privately. I was stressing this one day in a talk when a lady asked how this might apply to her, given that she was home with young children who demanded her total attention. "Where would I ever find an uninterrupted hour each day?" she moaned. "I would, I am afraid, be praying with children screaming and tugging at my pant legs."

A few years ago, I might have been tempted to point out to her that if her life was that hectic then she, of all people, needed time daily away from her children, for private prayer, among other things. As it is, I gave her different advice: "If you are home alone with small children whose needs give you little uninterrupted time, then you don't need an hour of private prayer daily. Raising small children, if it is done with love and generosity, will do for you exactly what private prayer does."

Left unqualified, this is a dangerous statement. In fact, it suggests that raising children is a functional substitute for prayer. However, in making the assertion that a certain service—in this case, raising children—in fact can be prayer, I am bolstered by the testimony of contemplatives themselves.

Carlo Carretto, one of our century's best spiritual writers, spent many years in the Sahara Desert by himself, praying. Yet he once confessed that he felt that his mother, who spent nearly thirty years raising children, was much more contemplative than he was, and less selfish. If that is true, the conclusion we should draw is not that there was anything wrong with Carretto's long hours of solitude in the desert, but that there was something very right about the years his mother lived an interrupted life amid the noise and demands of small children.

Certain vocations, such as raising children, offer a perfect setting for living a contemplative life. They provide a desert for reflection, a real monastery. The mother who stays home with small children experiences a very real withdrawal from the world. Her existence is certainly monastic. Her tasks and preoccupations remove her from the centers of social life and from the centers of important power. She feels removed. Moreover, her constant contact with young children gives her a privileged opportunity to learn empathy and unselfishness.

Perhaps more so than even the monk or the minister of the Gospel, she is forced, almost against her will, to mature. For years, while she is raising small children, her time is not her own, her own needs have to be put into second place, and every time she turns around some hand is reaching out demanding something. Years of this will mature most anyone.

CHAPTER FIVE

Growing to Maturity in Prayer

Patience with God

L IFE, AS WE can all attest, is not without its bitter frustrations and crushing heartaches. We all live with a lot of pain and unresolved tensions that can test the strongest faith and the stoutest heart. Who among us doesn't experience regularly the pain of sickness, various kinds of personal and professional failure, some kind of humiliation, the inadequacy of self-expression, the soul-searing losses of loved ones, every kind of frustrated longing, and the nagging pain of life's inadequacy? In this life, everything comes with shadow.

Jesus promised that the meek would inherit the earth, but mostly it doesn't seem that way. Only the arrogant among us believe that. There's a Ziggy cartoon that shows him praying to God in these words: "I just want to let you know that the meek are still getting clobbered down here!" Often that appears to be the case. So where is God? Where is the truth in Jesus's promise about the meek inheriting the earth? In the face of long-standing global injustice, we either live in a long-suffering patience with God or we come to believe that neither God's promises nor God's existence holds true.

When Jesus was dying on the cross, some onlookers were taunting him and challenging his message with the words: *If you are the Son of God, let him rescue you!* In essence: *If God is real and your message is true, prove it right now!* But God let Jesus die! The same held true for Jesus himself in the face of the death of Lazarus. Jesus was being challenged: *If you possess God's power in this world and you love this man, why don't you save him from dying?* But Jesus let Lazarus die! And the first community of disciples, immediately after the Ascension, painfully struggled with the same question: *Jesus is God and he loves us—so why does he let us die?*

Each of us asks that question in our own way because what we want is a God who rescues us, who intervenes actively for justice and goodness in this world, who acts visibly now in this life, and who doesn't let us get sick and die. None of us wants a God who asks us to live in a life-long patience, predicated on the promise that in the end, whenever that will be, love and justice will prevail, all tears will be dried, and all finally will be well. We want life, love, justice, and consummation now, not in some distant future and only after a lifetime of heartache. God, as a Jewish axiom puts it, is never in a hurry!

And so we live with a lot of expressed and unexpressed impatience with God. Atheists, it would seem, at a certain point just give up on playing the game and more or less say the words: *I've seen enough; I've waited enough; and it's not enough! I will no longer wait for God!* But if atheism is just another way of saying, "I will no longer wait for God," then the opposite is also true: faith is just another way of saying, "I will wait for God." If atheism is impatience, faith is patience.

Why the need for such great patience? Does God want to test us? Does God want to see if we indeed have a faith that is worthy of a great reward? No. God has no need to play such a game, and neither do we. It's not that God wants to test our patience. The need for patience arises out of the rhythms innate within life itself and within love itself. They need to unfold, as do flowers and pregnancies, according to their own good time. They cannot be rushed, no matter how great our impatience or how great our discomfort.

The Sustaining Power of Ritual

Never travel with anyone who expects you to be interesting all the time. On a long trip, there are bound to be some boring stretches.

That's an axiom offered by Daniel Berrigan in his book *Ten Commandments for the Long Haul*, and it contains a wisdom that is often absent today in our marriages, our family lives, our friendships, our churches, and our spiritual lives.

Today we often crucify others and ourselves with the impossible notion that inside of our relationships, our families, our churches, and our prayer lives we are meant to be alert, attentive, enthusiastic, and emotionally present all the time. We are never given permission to be distracted, bored, or anxious to move on to something else because we are weighed down with the pressures and tiredness of our own lives. We lay guilt on each other and on ourselves with these kinds of judgments: *Sometimes you're too distracted and tired to really hear me! You're not really present to this meal! You're bored at church! You're anxious to get this over with! You don't love me like you did at first! Your heart isn't in this as it used to be!*

While there is a healthy challenge in these judgments, they also betray a naiveté and lack of understanding of what actually sustains us in our daily lives. We've gone ritually tone-deaf.

What do I mean by that? Here's an example:

A recent study on marriage points out that couples who make it a habit to give each other a ritual embrace or kiss before leaving the house in the morning and another ritual embrace or kiss before retiring at night fare better than those who let this gesture be determined by simple spontaneity or mood. The study makes the point that even if the ritual kiss is done in a distracted, hurried, perfunctory, or duty-bound way, it still serves a very important function; namely, it speaks of fidelity and commitment beyond the ups and downs of our emotions, distractions, and tiredness on a given day. It is a ritual, an act that is done regularly, precisely to say what our hearts and heads cannot always say, namely, that the deepest part of us remains committed, even during those times when we are too tired or self-preoccupied to be as attentive and present as we should be. It says we still love the other and remain committed despite the inevitable changes and pressures the seasons bring.

This is often not understood today. An over-idealization of love, family, Church, and prayer often crucifies the reality. Popular culture would have us believe that love should be romantic, exciting, and interesting all the time, and that lack of felt emotion is a signal that something is wrong. Liturgists and prayer leaders would have us believe that every church service needs to be full of enthusiasm and emotion and that there is something wrong with us when we find ourselves flat, bored, looking at our wristwatches, and resisting emotional engagement during church or prayer. Everywhere we are warned about the dangers of doing something simply because it is duty, that there is something wrong when the movements of love, prayer, or service become routine. Why do something if your heart isn't in it?

Again, there is something legitimate in these warnings: duty and commitment without heart will not ultimately sustain themselves. But with that being admitted, it is important to recognize and name the fact that any relationship in love, family, church, or prayer can sustain itself over a long period only through ritual and routine. Ritual sustains the heart, not vice versa.

The same holds true for prayer. Anyone who prays only when she can affectively bring along her heart and soul will not sustain prayer for long. But the habit of prayer, the ritual, simple fidelity to the act, showing up to do it irrespective of feelings and mood, can sustain prayer for a lifetime and rein in the roaming of the head and heart.

Facing our Demons

We live lives of tortured complexity. Inside each of us there is both a saint and a sinner and enough complexity to write our own book on abnormal psychology. Our hearts are a murky caldron of grace and sin, angels and demons. Always, it seems, we are torn in a way that leaves us feeling unsure, guilty, and tense. It is no simple task being a human being.

Demons, Jesus tells us, are to be confronted in the desert. The desert is that place where one does battle with Satan. What exactly does that mean? Is Satan, the devil, to be conceived of as a personified force, a fallen archangel, Lucifer? Or is Satan a code name for that vast range of inner disturbances (addictions, scars, paranoia, fear, bitterness, and sexual wounds) that habitually torment us? What exactly are the principalities and powers that are beyond us?

That question is not so important here. Whether the devil is a person, an addiction, or a paranoia, in the end we still need to do battle at exactly the same place. Most of us are not called upon to confront the Satan of classical exorcisms. Rather, we meet Satan in the same way the prodigal son and his older brother met him: in weakness and bitterness. Ultimately these are the demons that must be met.

To go into the desert means to stare our inner chaos in the face. What demons live inside this chaos? The demons of the prodigal son and his older brother—the demons of grandiosity, loneliness, and unbridled sexuality, and the demons of paranoia, woundedness, and joylessness. What faces do these take?

Grandiosity is the demon that tells us we are the center of the universe, our lives are more important than those of others. This is a demon manifest in our daydreams, in those inner voices we hear, which always tell us that we are the special one, the superstar, the one singled out for greatness. This is the demon of self-preoccupation and self-centeredness, forever urging us to stand out, to be special.

Loneliness is the demon of unhealthy restlessness. This is a demon of fear, which torments us by telling us constantly that, at the end of the day, we will be alone, unloved, excluded, outside the circle. It makes us pathologically desperate, looking always for someone or something that can take our loneliness away.

Unbridled sexuality is the demon of obsession, addiction, and lust. It makes us believe that sex (or some such pleasure) is a panacea, the final salvation, or, if not that, at least the best this world can offer. It urges us to bracket everything else—sacred commitment, moral ideal, and consequences for ourselves and others—for a single, furtive pleasure. It is a demon with ten thousand faces, obsessing us all, whether we admit it or not.

Paranoia is the demon of bitterness, anger, and jealousy. It makes us believe that life has cheated us, that we have not been given our just place, that the celebration is always about others and never about us. This demon fills us with the urge to be cynical, cold, distrustful, and cursing.

Woundedness is the demon that tells us our innocence and wholeness are irretrievably broken and that, for us, it is too late. The best we can do now is to take consolation in comfort, food, drink, pornography, drugs, or some such thing.

Finally, the last demon in this family is that of *joylessness,* the demon of self-pity that tells us that joylessness is maturity, that cynicism is wisdom, and that bitterness is justice. This is the demon that keeps us from entering the room of celebration and joining the dance.

All of these demons are inside every one of us. To stare them in the face is to enter the desert. A scary thing? Yes, but the Scriptures assure us that, if we do muster the courage to face them, God will send angels to minister to us, and these angels will bring along calm, restfulness, patience, empathy, humility, solicitude, joy, playfulness, and humor.

Overcoming Anger

I remember a confession I heard as a young priest. It was just before a Eucharist and everyone was hurrying through the line, hoping for a two-minute confession, when a woman, somewhere in her fifties, knelt before me. Hers was not a regular confession, a quick listing of sins, but words to this effect:

> This is hard for me to talk about, and even just to admit, but lately I'm finding myself filling constantly with anger. It is hard to describe exactly, because it is not so much that certain things trigger it, but that I find myself growing bitter. I'm resentful at my husband and family because they take me so much for granted, and I am angry at the world, I guess, for the same reason. Also, and I don't understand this at all, I have resentments toward God. I can't word this exactly, but

I'm angry at God—angry about some things in my life, angry because life is so unfair at times, and angry that everything is so hopelessly the way it is. I don't understand this. I never was an angry person when I was younger, and now I'm filling with anger. How is it that now, when I am older, that I am getting more immature?

I assured her that hers was not the struggle of the immature, as she thought, but rather the struggle of the mature, the struggle of those who have conquered enough of the weaknesses of youth to come face to face with a bigger hurdle: the barrier of resentment.

Near the end of our lives, many of us struggle to move beyond the death of our dreams, beyond how we have been wounded and cheated, and beyond all the resentments that come with aging. This is one of the final tasks of the spiritual life: the movement from resentment to gratitude, from cursing to blessing, from bitterness to graciousness. And it is a monumental task.

There is a lot of anger in us as we get older. This is not a case of growing angry as we grow older, but of angry people growing older. Psychology tells us that we get our wounds early on in life, but our angers emerge later. When we are young, our energy and our dreams are still strong enough to shield us from the full brunt of our wounds, our hurts, and life's unfairness. I remember, as a young man of twenty, living in a seminary with nearly fifty young men my own age. We were all pretty immature, but strangely we lived together relatively well and peaceably. Today, if you would put those fifty persons together again in the same living situation we would, soon enough I suspect, kill each other. We are more mature now, but we are also full of the angers, disappointments, and resentments of midlife. Like the older brother of the prodigal son, we are now acutely aware that someone less deserving than we are gets to dance and eat the fatted calf.

This must be understood for what it is: not a sign of regression, but a critical new moment in the spiritual life. As we age and become ever more aware of our wounds, our wasted potential, and the unfairness of life, we come face to face with the final spiritual hurdle—the challenge to become mellow and gracious in spirit. The spiritual task of midlife and old age is that of wrestling with God, of acknowledging all of the ways in which life has disappointed and betrayed us and, in spite of that, understanding what God means with the words: "My child, everything I have is yours!"

The Dangers of Despair

Despair is something we misunderstand, just as we misunderstand the resurrection. Both are not experiences that are extraordinary, at the end of life. Resurrection and despair lie in the bread and butter of our existence.

Generally we tend to confuse despair with the type of illness that leads to suicide or pathological withdrawal. This is not despair. It is an illness, like heart disease, cancer, or high blood pressure. Despair has, I submit, nothing whatever to do with those souls, often of extraordinary sensitivity and goodness, who were unable to survive the world's emotional and psychological napalm. In their deaths there is, generally, no more guilt, sin, or freedom involved than there is in the death of a cancer or heart attack victim. In each case, the person dies against his or her own choice, unfree and unable to continue to live.

Real despair, like all of the worst demons, is infinitely more subtle. What is it? It is the death of our sense of surprise, the belief that nothing new can happen to us. We despair at that precise moment when, consciously or unconsciously, we say in resignation: "That is the way I am, that is the way things have always been for me, and that is the way it will always be. For me, it is too late!" Once this has been said, we are in a tomb. Much of us is dead, and more of us is still dying.

Why is this kind of despair dangerous? Because the resurrection is always, as it was the first time, a surprise—the totally unexpected, the impossible, and that which defies all logic, the laws of nature, and the wisdom of common sense and convention. When we have every angle of reality so calculated and figured that we know all the possibilities, then nothing new can come along to surprise us. Sadly, our prophecy then will be self-fulfilling because we have ceased believing in God and grace in a real sense. We have slimmed down God and grace to fit our own small minds. We live not merely in despair, but also in mediocrity.

Our world is not full of mediocre persons. It is full, rather, of extraordinarily gifted persons, living in mediocrity and in a subsequent frustration. And we are frustrated at all levels. Spiritually, we know we are lackluster. We pray seldom and poorly. We know we should, and could, make more effort, but we feel helpless against longstanding habits of laziness, dissipation, and distraction. Despite our good intentions, we have never really carried things through. We have despaired that we will become better people.

Interpersonally, it is much the same story: we are frustrated and mediocre. Entombed in longstanding habits of resentment and infidelity, shame and inhibition, we are prevented from being fully loving in warm, satisfying friendships with others. We are in deep tombs, behind a wall of stone. Worst of all, in the end, we have given up hope. We have said: "I've tried, but it didn't work! For me, it is too late."

The resurrection tells us it is never too late. Every so often we will be surprised. We must believe that the stone will be rolled back, and we must be ready to poke out our timid heads, take off the linen bindings of death, and walk free for a time, breathing resurrection air.

Wrestling with God

Nikos Kazantzakis, the author of *Zorba the Greek*, was an extraordinarily complex man, especially religiously. An artist, a searcher, strongly independent, yet a man with a mystical bent, he often found himself involved in painful interior struggles in his relationship with God. Sometimes he would acquiesce in obedience, other times he would hold out in proud resistance.

In his memoir, *Report to Greco*, he shares a personal story. As a young man, he spent a summer in a monastery during which he had a series of conversations with an old monk. One day he asked the old monk: "Do you still wrestle with the devil, Father Makários?" The monk answered, "Not any longer, my child. I have grown old now, and he has grown old with me. He doesn't have the strength...I wrestle with God."

There's a lot contained in that remark, "I wrestle with God." Among other things, it suggests that the struggles in later life can be very different from what we battle earlier on. In the normal pattern of things, we spend the first half of our lives struggling with sensuality, greed, and sexuality; we spend the last half of our lives struggling with forgiveness and anger. That anger is often, however unconsciously, focused on God. In the end, our real struggle is with God.

But wrestling with God has another aspect. It invites us to a certain kind of prayer. Prayer isn't meant to be a simple acquiescence to God's will. It's meant to be an acquiescence, yes, but a mature acquiescence, come to at the end of a long struggle.

We see this in the prayer of the great figures in Scripture: Abraham, Moses, the apostles, and Jesus. Abraham argues with God and initially talks him out of destroying Sodom; Moses at first resists his call, protesting that his brother is better suited for the job; the apostles excuse themselves for a long time before finally putting their lives on the line; and Jesus gives himself over in the Garden of Gethsemane only after first begging his Father for a reprieve. As Rabbi Abraham Joshua Heschel put it, from Abraham through Jesus we see how the great figures of our faith are not in the habit of easily saying: "Thy will be done!" but often, for a while at least, counter God's invitation with: "Thy will be changed!"

Struggling with God's will and offering resistance to what it calls us to can be a bad thing, but it also can be a mature form of prayer. The book of Genesis describes an incident in which Jacob wrestled with a spirit for a whole night, and in the morning that spirit turned out to be God. What a perfect icon for prayer! A human being and God, wrestling in the dust of this earth! Doesn't that accurately describe the human struggle?

We would do well to integrate this, the concept of wrestling with God, into our understanding of faith and prayer. We honor neither ourselves nor the Scriptures when we make things too simple. Human will doesn't bend easily, nor should it, and the heart has complexities that need to be respected, even as we try to rein in its more possessive longings. God, who built us, understands this and is up to the task of wrestling with us and our resistance. But we should lay out our hearts in honesty. Jesus did.

Love through Locked Doors

Several years ago, a family I know well lost a daughter through suicide. She was in her late twenties and had become dangerously depressed.

An initial attempt at suicide failed. The family then rushed around her. They brought her home, strove to be with her constantly, sent her to doctors and psychiatrists, and generally tried everything within their power to love and coax her out of her depression. It didn't work. Eventually, she succeeded in taking her own life.

Looking at her death and her family's efforts to love her and save her life, one sees how, at a certain point, human love can be helpless. Sometimes all the effort, patience, and love in the world cannot get through to a frightened, sick, depressed person. In spite of everything, that person remains locked inside herself, or himself, huddled against love, unfree, inaccessible, bent upon self-destruction. None of us who has ever dealt with a situation like this has been immune to the deep feelings of discouragement, guilt, hopelessness, and fear that ensue. Love, regardless of effort, seems powerless.

Fortunately, we are not without hope and consolation. We believe in the ultimate redeeming power of love, and in the power of a love beyond our own that can do that redeeming. God's love is not stymied in the same way as is ours. Unlike ours, it can go through locked doors, enter closed hearts, and breathe peace and new life into frightened, paralyzed persons. Our hope and our belief in this are expressed in one of the articles of our Apostles' Creed: "He descended into hell." What an incredible statement that is: God descended into hell. If that is true, and everything in Christ's life and teaching suggests it is, then the human heart has its ultimate consolation: Love will triumph.

We haven't always understood those words to mean that, however. The doctrine of Christ's descent into hell is first and foremost a doctrine about love, God's love for us, and the power of that love to go to all lengths, to descend to all depths, and to go through virtually every barrier to redeem a wounded, huddled, frightened, paranoid, alienated, and unfree humanity.

By dying as he did, Christ shows that he loves us in such a way that he can descend into our private hells. His love is so empathetic and compassionate that it can penetrate all barriers that we construct out of hurt and fear, in order to enter right into our despair and hopelessness. We see this idea expressed powerfully in John 20. Twice John presents the disciples as huddled behind closed doors, locked in because of fear. Twice John has Jesus come through the locked doors and stand in the midst of that frightened and depressed group and breathe peace into them. That image—Christ going through locked doors—is perhaps the most consoling image within our entire faith. Put simply, it means God can help us even when we cannot help ourselves. God can empower us even when we are too weak and despairing to even, minimally, open the door to let him in. That is not only consoling, it is also corrective of a bad spirituality on which many of us were raised.

Unlike our love, God's love is not left helplessly knocking at the door of fear, depression, hurt, and sickness. It does not require that a person, especially a sick person, first find the strength to make the initial move to open himself/herself up to health. In that lies our ultimate consolation. There is no hell—no private hell of wound, depression, fear, sickness, or even bitterness—that God's love cannot and will not descend into. Once there, it will breathe out the peace of the Holy Spirit.

God, our Real Mother

Recently, I attended a funeral of a young man, a relative of mine, who had been killed in an automobile accident. He was eighteen and recently had graduated from high school. A death like his is hard. How does one begin the impossible task of understanding such an accident? What words, if any, have use as consolation? When someone is struck down when life is really just beginning, even words about resurrection and eternal life can sound hollow. A compulsory disconsolateness takes over. One can only, as the author of Lamentations puts it, put one's mouth to the dust and wait.

Perhaps it is best not to speak too much at funerals. Our stuttering and our inarticulateness might say the most important things that need to be said: "I am here. I care. I'll suffer with you." And yet there is a need for words, some words—words that help clarify our relationship to the person we are burying and to the God in whom we believe. When someone close to us dies, especially a young person, we experience more than simple shock and hurt. We are left with feelings of guilt. At one level, we feel guilty because we go on living while someone else dies. At another level, a more painful one, we feel guilty about the incompleteness of our relationship with the person who has died, even if that relationship was essentially a good one.

Coupled with this, especially if the one who died is young, there are feelings of fear and anxiety. We sense an unfinishedness, an unreadiness, and even a certain brutality: "He is so young, so fragile still, so unprepared to give up life and to be so finally separated from home and friends." Like a mother who worries about her child when she or he first leaves home, we worry about the young who die. They are too tender still to be subjected to death, to irrevocable separation, to a terrifying newness, to a final judgment.

As we search among the strands of hope and grasp for something to hang onto in the face of such a death, perhaps we can do no better than to seize onto the words: *He is in better hands than ours.* Those are words of faith and they assure us that the God who gave this young man life—who gave him a gentle mother, a loving family and friends, who gave him exuberance and the lively life of the young—can be further trusted to bring that life to completeness and to bring him gently into life everlasting.

In understanding death, it is useful to look at birth. When a child is born, she or he is born into the arms and care of a mother. Save for the tremendous care, gentleness, and attention of a mother, a child is radically unready to live in this world. Given a mother, though, everything changes. There is some trauma in being born, but it is brief. Very quickly, the gentleness, patience, and tenderness of a mother erase the trauma of birth. In the care of a loving mother, the passage from birth to adulthood is not ungentle and traumatic, but a delightful adventure in awakening.

God is our real mother—more tender, more loving, and more understanding than any earthly mother. Our birth into eternal life through the birth canal of death must be seen just as our birth into this life. Just as here, in infancy, our mother was ever so tender and patient with us; in death, even more so, is God. The hands that receive us at death are not the rough hands of our world. The heart that embraces us there will not let anything be too much for us. We will, children that we are, be gently, understandingly, and tenderly guided and coaxed into eternal life. Being born into God's arms surely will be as gentle and tender an experience as was the experience of being born into our mother's arms.

CHAPTER SIX

Listening to God's Heartbeat

THE LAST SUPPER account in John's Gospel gives us a
wonderful mystical image. The evangelist describes the
Beloved Disciple as reclining on the breast of Jesus. What's
contained in this image? A number of things:

First, when you put your head upon someone else's chest, your
ear is just above that person's heart and you are able to hear his or
her heartbeat. Hence, in John's image, we see the Beloved Disciple
with his ear on Jesus's heart, hearing Jesus's heartbeat, and from
that perspective looking out into the world. This is John's ultimate
image for discipleship: The ideal disciple is the one who is attuned to
Christ's heartbeat and sees the world with that sound in his or her ear.

Then there is a second level to the image: It is an icon of peace, a
child at its mother's breast, contented, satiated, calm, free of tension,
not wanting to be anywhere else. This is an image of primal intimacy,
of symbiotic oneness, a connection deeper than romantic love.

And for John, it is also a Eucharistic image. What we see, in this
image of a person with his ear on Jesus's heart, is how John wants us
to imagine ourselves when we are at Eucharist because, ultimately,
that is what the Eucharist is—a physical reclining on the breast of
Christ. In the Eucharist, Jesus gives us, physically, a breast to lean on,
a place of safety and security from which to see the world.

This is also an image of how we should touch God and be sustained by him in solitude. Henri Nouwen once said that by touching the center of our solitude, we sense that we have been touched by loving hands. Deep inside each of us, like a brand, there is a place where God has touched, caressed, and kissed us. Long before memory, long before we ever remember touching or loving or kissing anyone or anything, or being touched by anything or anybody in this world, there is a different kind of memory, the memory of being gently touched by loving hands. When our ear is pressed to God's heart—to the breast of all that is good, true, and beautiful—we hear a certain heartbeat and we remember, remember in some inchoate place, at a level beyond thought, that we were once gently kissed by God.

Archetypally this is what's deepest within us. There is an ancient legend that holds that when an infant is created, God kisses its soul and sings to it. As its guardian angel carries the soul to earth to join its body, she also sings to it. The legend says God's kiss and his song, as well as the song of the angel, remain in that soul forever—to be called up, cherished, shared, and to become the basis of all of our songs. But to feel that kiss, to hear that song, requires solitude. You do not feel gentleness when inside of you and all around you there is noise, abrasiveness, anger, bitterness, jealousy, competitiveness, and paranoia. The sound of God's heartbeat is audible only in a certain solitude and in the gentleness it brings.

John of the Cross once defined solitude as "bringing the mild into harmony with the mild." That was his way of saying that we will begin to remember the primordial touch of God when, through solitude, we empty our hearts of all that is not mild: noise, anger, bitterness, and jealousy. When we become mild, we will remember that we have been touched by loving hands and, like the Beloved Disciple, we then will have our ear to the heartbeat of Christ.

Inside each of us there is a church, an oratory, a place of worship, a sanctuary not made by human hands. And it is a gentle place, a virgin place, a holy place, a place where there is no anger, no sense of being cheated, no need to be competitive, and no need to be restless. It is a soft place; but it can be violated, through a giving of oneself that does not respect oneself, and, especially, through lying and rationalizing and the cauterization, warping, and hardening of heart that follow upon that. Conversely, though, it is also a place that can remain inviolate, sacred, and untouched, even when abused and violated. It is in that place, entered into through solitude and gentleness of spirit, that we have a privileged access to God, because that is the place where God has already touched us and where we, however dimly, remember that.

We were once touched by hands far gentler and more loving than our own. The memory of that touch is a brand: warm, dark, gentle. To enter that memory is to lean on the breast of Christ, just as the Beloved Disciple did at the Last Supper. From that place, with our ear on Christ's heart, we have the truest perspective on our world.

Resting in God's Presence

1. Choose a place where you can sit quietly, comfortably, for fifteen minutes or more. If it will help you relax, set a timer so you will know when it is time to end your prayer.
2. Read a short passage of Scripture or some other spiritual reading, such as one of the brief reflections in this book, then put the reading aside.
3. Close your eyes or focus your gaze on a candle flame, a beautiful icon, or a peaceful image. Imagine yourself in the presence of God, a God who yearns to be close to you. Some people find it helpful to silently repeat a simple word or phrase: "Jesus." "Blessed be God." "Hosanna." "Lord, have mercy."

If you begin to feel anxious or to worry that you are not "doing it right," remember the words of a holy peasant who, when asked to share his secret to deep prayer, said simply, "I just look at God, and I let God look at me." Anyone who has ever been in love will know the power of those words. It is enough to be relaxed and quiet in the presence of God, ready to receive and to return God's loving glance.

Also by Ronald Rolheiser

Books

Against an Infinite Horizon: The Finger of God in Our Everyday Lives (New York: Crossroad, 2002)

Forgotten Among the Lilies: Learning to Love Beyond Our Fears (New York: Image, 2007)

The Holy Longing: The Search for a Christian Spirituality (New York: Doubleday, 1999)

Our One Great Act of Fidelity: Waiting for Christ in the Eucharist (New York: Image, 2011)

The Restless Heart: Finding Our Spiritual Home in Times of Loneliness (New York: Doubleday, 2004)

The Shattered Lantern: Rediscovering a Felt Presence of God (New York: Crossroad, 2005)

Audio

Against an Infinite Horizon: The Finger of God in Our Everyday Lives (Cincinnati: Franciscan Media, 2003)

Forgotten Among the Lilies: Learning to Love Beyond Our Fears (Cincinnati: Franciscan Media, 2005)

The Holy Longing: The Search for a Christian Spirituality (Cincinnati: Franciscan Media, 2003)

Our One Great Act of Fidelity: Waiting for Christ in the Eucharist (Cincinnati: Franciscan Media, 2013)

The Restless Heart: Finding Our Spiritual Home in Times of Loneliness (Cincinnati: Franciscan Media, 2004)

The Shattered Lantern: Rediscovering a Felt Presence of God (Cincinnati: Franciscan Media, 2003)

Newsletters

Agony in the Garden: Understanding the Passion of Jesus, Catholic Update, February 2008.

The Abundance of God and Our Christian Response, Catholic Update, June, 2011.

. . . .

There is a study guide available for *Prayer: Our Deepest Longing*, which can be used by either individuals or small groups to further explore the concepts and ideas that will help you establish a deeper, more meaningful prayer life. Go to www.FranciscanMedia.org/guide to download this free resource.